THERE IS MORE TO BUSINESS THAN MARKETING AND SALES!

What Else Business Owners Need To Know To Be Successful

By

Judi Craig, Ph.D., MCC
Executive & Business Coach

First printing September 2012

Printed in the United States of America
ISBN 978-0-9705648-5-6

ACKNOWLEDGMENTS

My thanks go to Domenic Fusco for his creative cover design—and to my dear friend, Carol Rice, for her perceptive editing.

And, of course, to my husband, Jim Norris, for his continued encouragement and love.

INTRODUCTION

When you hear the statistics about how many start-up businesses fail, it's depressing. And did you know that less than one half of one percent of small business owners ever reach one million dollars in revenue? And that less than 30 percent make more than $100,000 annually?

It seems there are a zillion books telling business owners how to succeed—most focusing on marketing and sales know-how. But as an executive and business coach, I've noticed that there are many other factors at stake in determining if a business will or won't derail—and they are all within the business owner's control. They have to do with people and communication skills, the ability to manage time effectively, and the knowledge of how to engage and motivate employees while making them accountable.

Whether you're a business owner in retail or a professional offering a service, read on to discover those "missing pieces".

6

TABLE OF CONTENTS

BEING A GREAT BOSS

As a business owner, you are the ultimate boss—the leader of your company or professional practice. Whether you have many employees or just one, it is you who becomes the role model and sets the tone for your business. How long you keep your employees—and your ultimate success or failure—depends in large part on what kind of boss you are.

Listening to employee complaints—whether in the lunch room or in exit interviews—it's pretty clear what kind of boss they really want. Follow these guidelines and people who work for you will want to come to work in the mornings and give you their best efforts.

Set Clear Expectations

If there's one thing that will drive employees crazy, it is a boss who is not clear about what she expects. Language is a tricky thing, and what is perfectly clear to you can be perceived quite differently by others.

Let's imagine that you say, "I'd like this to be ready to roll out as soon as possible." Your definition of "soon" may not be anywhere near the same as the other person's. The employee may figure next week will be fine, but what you really meant was "I need this tomorrow!"

What can help clarify matters is for you to ask the other person to recap what has been stated. If *you* do the recapping, the other person may nod agreement but still have a totally different idea about what is expected. For example, remember when a teacher explained something to you and then asked if you understood it? You said 'yes" even when you didn't have a clue? But if the teacher had asked you to repeat the instructions, she would have known whether or not you really understood what she had just explained. So if you ask the *employee* to do the recapping, you'll get a clear idea about whether or not you and he are on the same page.

It is best to first explain first explain the concept of recapping to your employees—and why you will be asking them to do it. They you can simply say "Will you recap that for me?"

It is important that your expectations are clearly stated, including the roles and responsibilities of your employees. You want people to know what it is they are supposed to do to be successful in their jobs.

Let People Do Their Jobs

The smart boss will hire good people and then give them the freedom to do their jobs without micromanaging them. How much you need to supervise depends on the skill level, the experience and the reliability of the employee.

You will be wise to check in with your employees about the level of supervision you are providing. Some actually may want you to give them greater direction. Others may ask for more freedom and, if you can't give it to them, you need to explain your reasons.

Be Approachable

The boss who makes sure the door to her office is open at least some time during the day will encourage employees with questions or concerns to drop by. But the open door won't do it by itself. You also need to convey with your facial expression and body language that you are willing to listen rather than seeming impatient and put-out by the visit. Better to state frankly that you cannot be available at that moment—and schedule another time when you will be available—than to be preoccupied and listen half-heartedly.

Also, you want to be sure to make it easy for your employees to tell you bad news without 'shooting the messenger'. If not, people will tell you only what they think you want to hear rather than letting you know what is really going on. Encourage those difficult conversations by remaining calm even when listening to information that is upsetting.

Be On Time

When the boss doesn't honor her time commitments and consistently runs late for her appointments and meetings, she gives the message that only her time is important. The unspoken message is that other people's time doesn't really count.

If you lead a meeting, delegate someone else to start things off if you are running late. If you get behind on your schedule, call ahead either to cancel an appointment or to let the employee know to show up at a later time. Employees see this behavior as considerate and a sign of respect.

Ask For Feedback

The boss who asks his employees to give him honest feedback invites a trusting, collaborative atmosphere. You might ask "How can I support you better?", "What would you like to see me do differently that would make your job easier (more interesting, more fun, etc.)?" "Do you have some feedback for me about my role in that project?"; "How can I be of help to you?" Then, of course, your job is to listen without becoming defensive.

Tell The Truth

A boss who is reluctant to give an employee honest feedback for fear of being disliked or of hurting an employee's feelings is not doing himself, the business or the employee any favors. It often happens that an employee continues the same negative behavior year after year but continues to receive highly favorable performance appraisals. When that employee gets a boss who tells it like it is or, worse yet, gets fired, she feels betrayed and angry.

Part of your job as a boss involves taking responsibility to ensure an employee's success to whatever extent is possible—and that means giving honest feedback.

Encourage Employees To Take Charge Of Their Careers

A good boss will encourage employees to be proactive about getting what they need to advance in their career. If they want to advance in their careers, they need to be ready to ask for opportunities to keep up with new developments so they don't fall behind.

If you don't challenge your employees to grow, you invite poor morale and burn-out. Give them opportunities to enrich their skills through conferences, training, coaching, and mentoring.

Hold Yourself — And Others — Accountable

An effective boss doesn't allow employees to sidestep their responsibilities or accept their excuses for not delivering on a commitment. Let your employees know up-front how you will track or measure their successes as well as what to expect if their objectives aren't met. At the same time, be sure to hold yourself accountable by doing what you say you will do.

Motivate With Positives

You don't have to be charismatic, a cheerleader, or a motivational speaker to be a good boss. But you do need to focus on finding solutions to challenges rather than just complaining, blaming, or intimidating. Your positive attitude shows when you ask "How can we get there?", "What can we do to make this work?" or "What can we do differently next time to ensure success?" It's wise to use incentives for work well done rather than threats of what will happen if it isn't done correctly.

Take Personal Responsibility.

A good boss will always ask herself how *her* behavior might have contributed to a problem rather than criticizing everyone else. Even when it appears that someone else is 95 percent responsible for an error, it's always good to look for that 5 percent contribution that you might have made to the situation. What could you have done that you didn't do? What did you do that you should not have? Hindsight can be an excellent teacher and lead to better outcomes in the future.

Openly admit it when you make a mistake. This actually endears you to your employees because it gives them permission not to be terrified of making mistakes themselves.

Be Collaborative.

A good boss seeks input from others about decisions that will affect them. Instead of the "I'll tell you to jump and you ask how high" approach, be inclusive and get feedback from others before making decisions. When your employees know that you value their opinions, they have more buy-in to the decisions that are made and are more motivated to make sure they work.

Walk The Talk

If a boss asks his employees to follow certain procedures and to honor certain values, he needs to do the same. If you define the values for your business, you can't expect everyone else to follow them if you don't demonstrate them yourself. If you value "respect", you must be respectful. If you espouse "open communication", you must communicate openly. If you ask people not to gossip, you shouldn't gossip. If you ask your employees to read and act on their emails daily, you need to do likewise. If you tell them that it is important to have a positive attitude, then you must model the same.

Encourage Others To Have A Life Outside Of Work.

A good boss wants her employees to have a healthy balance between work and family responsibilities. You want people to go home on time and to take their earned vacations. And you model this by taking vacations yourself and by not working evenings or weekends on a routine basis.

Acknowledge Generously

Most employees feel overworked and under-appreciated. They become unmotivated or even angry if all they get is criticism. It's important to spot them doing something "right" and notice it. Recognition can be formal (a recognition banquet or ceremony), but even more important is spontaneous recognition for the "little things" — handling an angry customer well, staying late to finish a project, troubleshooting an issue before it becomes a crisis, meeting a deadline early, accomplishing a frustrating task. A compliment by email, recognition in a meeting, or a word of thanks can do wonders to improve both morale and commitment.

YOUR VISION AND MISSION

Every business owner begins with a vision, an idea of what he wants his business to accomplish, as well as thoughts of how he intends to bring the vision to fruition (the mission). As he begins to hire employees, it is critical that these ideas are written and well-articulated. A vision and mission statement will serve as a psychological magnet, drawing employees together with a unified goal.

A vision is *the big goal*, and often realistically unattainable. For Microsoft, it might be "A PC in every home". The vision is audacious; obviously, there will be other computer brands. But because it is audacious, it is inspiring. It's the "if you could wave a magic wand, what would you want to have happen?" goal.

The mission, in contrast, spells out how the business will work toward the vision—the actual doable steps that will be taken to move toward the vision. If the vision for an animal rescue group is "Make our city a no-kill city", the mission might be "We will provide shelter for 100 dogs until they are adopted into loving homes, as well as offer classes to the public on proper pet care and training."

If you are a solopreneur, you may think it's not really necessary to write a vision and mission for yourself, but do so anyway. It's an exercise that can help you get crystal clear about your business goals.

If you've never formally developed a vision and mission statement—or it's time for a revision—it's ideal to get every employee involved (whether one or many). This inclusive strategy lets the employees know that their ideas are valued and creates buy-in for the end product.

Call a meeting and begin with creating the vision statement. It should be brief and, remember, audacious. Ask your employees questions like "Why are we in this business?", "If we could wave a wand, what would be an outrageous goal for us?" As people respond, list their ideas on a whiteboard or flipchart until people come to a group consensus and are happy about the result.

Now move on to create the mission statement. Ask questions like "What do we need to actually do to move toward our vision?" and "What are the actions we need to take?", "What are the words we need to include in our statement?" Continue asking "What else needs to be included?" until the group has no more offerings.

Now ask the group to begin putting the words and phrases together to make the mission statement. As sentences are written for all to see, encourage changes until everyone is satisfied with the finished product.

Consider posting your vision and mission statement in your lobby or reception area. Include it on your brochure, website, or any other marketing materials.

But remember, the main reason you have created your vision and mission statement is to provide direction, clarity, and inspiration for your employees.

THE FACE OF YOUR BUSINESS

We all know that first impressions count for a lot. That's why as an astute business person, you will have business cards, brochures, and stationery that convey a professional look. But don't forget about your physical place of business. As soon as someone walks through the door, it's the lobby or reception area that is the face of your business.

What is the general "feel" you want your waiting area to convey? High end professionalism? A casual, home-like look? A no-nonsense, utilitarian appeal? Formal or informal?

While you want your lobby or reception area to reflect something about you and your type of business, you'll also want to consider the type of customers or clients you have. What type of environment will make them feel most comfortable? What is their level of education, income and sophistication?

Consider the following example: A dentist catered specifically to low-income, less educated clients. His wife, an equestrian, decorated his office and filled his coffee table with copies of Harvard Business Review, Fortune, Architectural Digest and magazines for thoroughbred horse breeders. Not a good match!

You'll want to make sure that you offer reading material that will be of interest to your visitors and that the offerings are current. If you have magazines in your waiting area from 2005, what do you think it says about you? Inattentive? Not current? Overwhelmed? Not organized? Best to get rid of anything that is over two month's old unless, of course, it's a collectible (for example, a series of National Geographics or reading material you have published).

For articles specifically about you or your business, consider having them nicely reproduced, framing them and hanging them on the wall for everyone to notice. In the media all the time? How about using a bulletin board where current articles can be posted?

Many businesses offer a continuously running educational video in their waiting rooms that describes the various services offered. If there are several professionals sharing an office who have different specialties, a video introducing each one and describing their expertise is a nice touch.

Having small individually wrapped candies or mints on a table, at the receptionist's area or counter or at the place where people check out and pay their bills increases your hospitality factor. If you are a solo professional or have just a few colleagues sharing office space and you see clients by appointment, letting your receptionist offer water, a soft drink, coffee or tea makes people feel welcome. For high-end clientele, china rather than Styrofoam or paper containers conveys a sense of elegance. In a larger waiting room that holds many customers at a time, consider installing a drinking fountain or water cooler.

If you have children who are clients or clients who bring their children with them, consider having a children's corner in your waiting room--or at least a basket with several children's books or magazines. If you do put toys in this area, make sure they are quiet and do not have small parts that can be scattered about. Children's tables with built-in games that can't be removed are ideal. A well-maintained aquarium is entertaining for children and restful for adults. Older youngsters may like listening to children's stories on CD—with headphones, of course.

Many offices have background music playing in the lobby. In addition to adding to the ambiance, this can also reduce the chance that people can overhear conversations at the reception desk or in the offices beyond.

Clean walls and good lighting will make any waiting area cheerier, and a fresh coat of paint can work wonders in brightening a dingy room. Real plants create more warmth than do artificial ones. And fresh flowers are always appealing.

Remember, what's hanging on the walls tells people something about you, so make sure it conveys the message that you intend. Even more important, make sure you don't have something on your walls that could offend the kinds of clients you see. Stay away from political or religious themes (unless your business is political or religious) and watch out for humor that some people would find offensive.

PEOPLE SKILLS

No matter how bright, how creative, how diligent, how experienced, how expert, or how well-intended you are, your success in the business world relies heavily on your "people skills."

Here are some tips to keep yours in prime shape!

Be a Good Listener

Nothing is more frustrating than talking to someone who isn't listening. Good listeners don't interrupt, don't multitask when they're listening, and don't just wait for the other person to take a breath so they can jump in and make their own points. They make eye contact and they don't fidget or act distracted during a conversation. They are comfortable with silence, allowing the other person to process her own thoughts. And they give the other person feedback about what's been said to show understanding, or they ask for clarification.

Be Friendly

People like a business owner who is friendly. He greets others when he walks past them, makes eye contact, and smiles often. He shows that he is concerned about what's on other people's minds and lives, not just about what is going on in his own. He places a higher priority on being interested rather than being interesting. He takes the time to know some personal things about his employees (the names of their spouse and children, their hobbies, what they like to read or watch on television, what they collect, etc.)—and brings those things up when appropriate so others know that he knows.

Seek Out Other People

It's important to initiate contact with other people rather than always waiting for them to come to you. Even if your job requires that you spend a lot of time in your office, take a few moments to make contact with people while you're on the way to the water cooler, the restroom, the fax or someone else's office. Take your breaks in the break room sometimes; eat lunch with others rather than at your own computer. Don't hole up in your office for an entire day.

Let People Know You

Even if you consider yourself to be a private person or an introvert, people want to know something about you on a more personal level. This doesn't mean you have to share your entire life story or talk about things you'd rather keep private. But a little self-disclosure, when appropriate, makes you more human and approachable as a business owner.

It can be as simple as coming into the office and saying, "Did you see that game last night on TV—it was really exciting!", "My daughter was in a fencing tournament this weekend", "I had a miserable golf game yesterday", "I got a new Bar-B-Q grill and was up half the night assembling the darn thing!" It's a matter of letting people know you have a life other than at work and makes you more human.

Be Non-defensive

When you get negative feedback, get blamed for something you didn't do, or feel you're being dealt with unfairly, it's important not to shut down communication by becoming defensive. This means that you don't rush to explain yourself, no matter how tempted you might be to do so. Instead, take your time, ask questions to clarify what the other person is saying to you, and then thank them for sharing the information (even if you don't agree with it). If you're furious, shocked or dismayed, tell the other person you'd like to think about what they've said and then get back to them. Acknowledge your own responsibility for whatever has gone wrong, even if you think someone else is 95 percent responsible for the problem. It is very attractive to show that you take personal responsibility for negatives as well as positives.

Deal With Your Feelings

We all have emotions, but the workplace is not the appropriate setting for emotional excesses or "dumps." Never send an email when you're angry. Give yourself a "time out" if you're upset, even if it means telling someone "I'm really upset right now; let me get back to you" or "Let's discuss this later this afternoon so I can clear my thoughts." Temper fits are a no-no. If you're having a bad day, it helps to tell those who work with you a bit about what's wrong, if appropriate, so they don't think you're upset with them.

Assert Yourself

There is a continuum of behavior that goes
from being passive to being assertive to being
aggressive. You want to stay in the "assertive" range.
That means that you speak your mind but that you do
so tactfully and without any emotional "charge" to
your communication. If you remain passive you deal
yourself out of decision-making; if you become
aggressive you alienate others. You want to be able to
be direct without being abrupt. You don't want to
come across as always having to be right. Most
important, you don't want to make others wrong
either by attack or by innuendo.

HOW'S YOUR EQ?

We all grew up familiar with the concept of IQ, our Intelligence Quotient. More recently, we're hearing a lot about EQ, our Emotional Quotient (also referred to as EI or Emotional Intelligence). It has to do with how well you manage your own--and others'--emotions.

EQ is the combination of interpersonal skills that allows you to read people and situations accurately. It lets you know when to speak up and when to remain silent, when to push and when to concede, when to negotiate and when not to. It's EQ that helps you understand how to de-escalate sticky situations, how to calm people down, how to empathize. It allows you to know what your "gut feeling" is and how best to deal with it.

While you might image that EQ is important in your personal relationships, it is also a critical component of business success. Numerous studies show that you have to have a high EQ if you're going to be a leader: Many bright, talented people fail to rise to the level of success they desire because they lack this important resource.

So what, exactly, is EQ? What are the skills?

Emotional Self-Awareness

Are you able to notice your feelings, to label them appropriately and to connect them to their sources? People who have high emotional self-awareness know what's going on inside their own skins and automatically question themselves about *why* they are feeling a particular way.

Emotional Expression

Can you express your feelings and your gut-level instincts? To be able to tell others how you feel and why saves time, strengthens connections with others, and enhances individual and group performance. Many people feel comfortable expressing only one or two emotions, but not the full range. For instance, you may be able to let others know when you are sad but not be able to tell them when you are angry.

Emotional Awareness of Others

Can you sense or intuit what other people are feeling from their words or body language? Do you pick up on another person's emotional energy, sense their moods, and notice specific cues that give you insight into what's going on with them?

Intentionality

Do you act deliberately "on purpose" to say what you mean and mean what you say? How consciously do you make decisions consistent with your personal and professional goals and values? When you act with intentionality, you accept responsibility for both your actions and your motivations. You remain focused on your objectives and you are aware of your deeply felt motivations for achieving them.

Creativity

Do you tap into multiple non-cognitive resources to help you think of new ideas, come up with alternative solutions to problems, and find effective new ways of doing things? How well can you brainstorm unusual approaches to problems or challenges? Thinking creatively means calling upon multiple sources: Your feelings, memories, hunches, and gut-level responses.

Resilience

When you face a difficult situation, how well do you bounce back from it? How flexible are you? Can you retain a sense of hopefulness and curiosity about the future even in the face of adversity? The opposite of resilience is rigidity: An inability to shift away from your conventional approach that may no longer work well in a specific situation.

Interpersonal Connections

Do you create and sustain a network of people with whom you can be your real self, to whom you can express appreciation and caring, and with whom you can share your vulnerabilities and hopes? Can you relate to others openly and honestly, asking for help when you need it?

Creative Discontent

Can you stay calm, focused, and emotionally grounded even when you face disagreement or conflict? Are you comfortable remaining true to your own personal boundaries while remaining open to new ideas? The opposite of creative discontent is destructive content: Hurrying toward false harmony and cutting off healthy disagreements.

Outlook

Are you a "glass is half full" or a "glass is half empty" person? Optimism is a fundamental confidence that things will go well in your life and has a high correlation with health, happiness, performance, successful relationships, and problem-solving capability. Can you say "I like who I am" and "I love my life"?

Compassion

Can you appreciate and value another person's point of view? Can you be forgiving to yourself as well as others? Can you "walk in another's shoes"? Can you suspend your judgments of others who are different from you and be sensitive to their feelings, even if you ultimately disagree with their position?

Intuition

Do you notice, trust, and actively use your hunches, gut-level feelings, and other non-cognitive responses produced by your senses? Neuroscientists tell us that the highest reasoning requires emotion and intuition, not just sequential analysis or technical rationality.

Trust Radius

Do you basically go through the world expecting to be able to trust other people until and if they prove otherwise? The ability to have a broad trust radius helps to suspend narrow judgment, enlist support and influence, and save time by harnessing the energy of those around you.

Personal Power

Do you believe that you basically have what it takes to meet life's challenges and create the life you choose? This skill is an inner knowing, a calm conviction about who you are and about your ability to get the things you want and need in your life. People high in personal power can—and do—set the direction in their lives.

Integrated Self

Do your intellectual, emotional, spiritual, and creative selves fit together to provide an integrated picture of who you are? This requires a highly developed state of awareness about your own beliefs and values, and reveals itself in behaviors that support those beliefs and values. This skill provides you with an inner guide that makes it easier to decide "the right thing to do" when conflicting values pull at you.

****

Now that you have an idea of what is involved in EQ, what if you sense that yours needs some beefing up? There is good news: All of the factors mentioned above are skills that can be learned. The critical step is to pick an area of weakness and consciously decide to work on it. Then, from a trusted colleague or friend who knows your interactions at work, ask for feedback about how you're doing.

But sometimes this isn't enough. You may be carrying some emotional baggage from your past that interferes with your best intentions, particularly if you have trust issues. A psychotherapist can help.

DELEGATION 101!

As a small business owner, you're in a leadership position. Delegation is an essential skill to master. But why?

First, it's going to be essential for your own time management to be able to delegate tasks to others. In your role, you're just going to get busier. You need to concentrate on the tasks that require your special expertise. If you're working at night, taking work home and/or working on the weekends, chances are that you need some help to preserve your sanity, your health—and probably your relationship with your significant other.

Second, delegation is a way to help others in your organization broaden their skill sets. How are you going to develop future leaders if you don't give them the experiences they need to grow in their careers?

But some of you may have a personality style that makes letting go difficult. It's likely you say, "It's just easier to do it myself" or "Nobody can do it right the way I want it done!" If this sounds familiar, you need to ask yourself, "What is the very best use of my time?" It's probably not making copies, sending out faxes, inputting routine data into a system, doing bookkeeping, answering the phone every time it rings, scheduling—well, you get the idea.

So let's say you're convinced that it would be a good idea for you to learn to delegate. How do you start?

First, take a couple of days and write a list of all of your daily work tasks. Then go through the list and highlight any that absolutely *require you* to do them—either because you're the only one with the expertise or there's some regulatory requirement that insists that the job be done only by you. For example, an attorney has to appear in a court of law; she can't send her paralegal or another staff person who is not an attorney. Arguing a case in court is not delegatable (unless there's another attorney in her practice who is qualified).

Next, look through the rest of the list and put a star by any task that you find boring or just dislike— you know, the things you put off, the ones that aren't exciting to you. Decide, if at all possible, to delegate these.

Look at your remaining tasks and ask yourself if any of them are duties that are typically done by people who make less money than you. For instance, do you frequently fax or copy documents when you have staff whose job it is to do those things? These are no-brainers to give up.

Now ask your direct reports, team members or the people you work closely with, "What do you see me doing that you would like to know more about for your own career development?" In other words, invite them to take charge of their own careers by allowing you to begin mentoring them on tasks they are either interested in or need to strengthen. In this way, you encourage their professional development while freeing yourself up to do more of the things that you want or need to do for your own business success.

Don't forget to ask your support staff this important question: "What do you see me doing at work that surprises you—that you logically think should be someone else's job?" Receptionists and secretaries usually hit the nail on the head when they are given permission to tell you what they see you doing that does (or should) fall in someone else's job description.

Once you've created the list of items that you're going to delegate—and figured out who you're going to delegate them to—there are a few ground rules that will help you be successful. If you simply assign someone a task with only a brief explanation and without a specific follow-up process, chances are the person will come back with something that doesn't begin to meet your expectations. While this gives you a great opportunity to say to yourself, "See, I knew I should do this instead of relying on someone else!", what you've really done is "dumped" rather than delegated! It's short-changing the other person not to give him a thorough explanation of exactly what it is you want done; you've set him up for probable failure.

It's also very important to establish an accountability process for the items you've delegated. If the job is very new to someone, you may want her to check in with you on a daily basis. But if you've given a task to someone you know has experience in that area and always meets deadlines, you can say something like "Just check in with me if you run into any problems."

One more thing: You'll want to be sure to determine a deadline for the task or, in the case of a big project, a deadline for each of the steps along the way. Deadlines can be changed, if necessary, but having them increases the level of commitment and provides a ready structure for tracking and accountability. Not having them leads to procrastination and excuses.

After all, you are still the person responsible for the end result. You want to insure success both for yourself and for the other person. The bonus? You'll have more time to be working *on* your business rather than *in* your business!

GETTING ORGANIZED

Take a look around your office. Do you see stacks of papers on your desk, bookshelves, credenza—even, Heaven forbid—the floor? Does your computer look like a kite that's about to take off because you have so many sticky notes attached to it as your reminder not to forget something (of course, after the fifth one, you never even look at them!)?

Now you may be saying to yourself "But I can find anything I need, so what's the problem?" Unfortunately, studies show that sometimes you can't. Even if you do find what you're looking for, it typically takes much longer than it does for people who have a well-organized office.

But that's not the main reason to get organized. Truth is, having stacks of work (or any kind of clutter) around you results in a psychological feeling of overwhelm. If a friend calls with a last-minute lunch invitation to hear a great speaker, are you likely to accept with all that visible evidence of unfinished work? Probably not. So you can miss out on a lot of opportunities. Who knows, maybe you would have met your next big client.

Worse yet, you never truly feel "finished" at the end of the day. Nagging thoughts about what hasn't been done creep into your mind during the evening (and maybe when you're tossing and turning while trying to go to sleep).

And what about your professional image? Are your clients and/or employees likely to look around and think "Gee, I wonder if my stuff will get lost?" Let's face it, the mess is not likely to inspire confidence in your capabilities.

Now some of you are thinking "But for me, out of sight is out of mind; I need to have all my work where I can see it or I'll forget about it."   If this sounds familiar, challenge yourself to experiment with cleaning everything up for a month or two and *then* take a look at the consequences on your productivity.

So you decide to take a day (or two) and get organized. Where do you start?

First, get a box of leaf bags and fill them with all the things you no longer need. This includes outdated files that don't need to be archived and out-of-date information. Look first where the dust is and work your way out from there.

Next, take a look at your office arrangement. Is your desk where you want it to be? How about bookshelves, the credenza and other furniture? This is the perfect time to re-think your flow of work and what will be the best arrangement for you. If you want your space to be more open and inviting, consider putting your desk in a corner so that when you're not working, you can turn and face the people who are visiting without having the desk between the two of you.

After doing whatever rearranging makes sense, look at what's "out" that shouldn't be. Do you need more file cabinets? Shelves? Storage boxes?

Are there changes you would like to make to your filing system? Don't despair—you don't have to take everything out of your file cabinets and start over. Just decide on your new system and begin implementing it; as you use a file from the old system, make it consistent with the new.

Now consider where your files are located. Which ones do you really need in your office? Can some be stored elsewhere in the building? The files you refer to *daily* need to be within reach while you are at your desk. This would include a "messages" file, perhaps one marked "urgent", reference lists (phone numbers of employees, menus from places where you order lunch), personal items (your child's soccer schedule), perhaps current projects or client files. Items that you are not using daily but are still current can be placed in file cabinets elsewhere in the room. If you just have to have something left out, place it in a file sorter on your desk or nearby space.

The idea is that you want to arrive at your office every day and see *nothing* on your desk except your telephone, computer, calendar and other essential equipment and *nothing* on your tables and shelves but decorative items.

Okay, so you clean everything up and get your office looking spiffy. You fixed the problem—but you haven't *resolved* it. Your office will look the way it did before in a week or two unless you create a *system* to maintain the changes. The simplest is to take the last five minutes before you leave your office for the day and put everything in its place. Viola!

One final thing: Once you've done all that hard work, why not celebrate by purchasing something for your office that will remind you of your accomplishment? Whether it is a ten-dollar mouse pad or an expensive piece of art, you'll get a great feeling every time you see it and know why it is there.

BATCHING

Are you looking for a proven way to increase your efficiency and get more work done during the day? Think one word: "Batch"!

The idea is to group all of your similar tasks together rather than spreading them throughout your day. Take email, for example. Many of us have been slaves to that familiar "you've got mail!" sound. We're working away, hear the sound and immediately turn to our computer screens to see who is emailing us. Or we visit our email inboxes throughout the day whenever we have a couple minutes. Either way, we wind up continually interrupting ourselves, decreasing our productivity and possibly going home late.

But what if, instead, you planned to check your email a couple times a day and actually *scheduled* that time in your calendar—just like a "real" appointment? Let's say you pick 8:30 in the morning when you first arrive at the office and 3 in the afternoon. Depending on the number of emails you receive most days, you might plan to spend ten to thirty minutes dealing with them during those pre-scheduled times. Of course, depending on your type of business, you might plan to check more often each day, or only once. No matter how many email breaks you plan to have, the idea is to schedule them and not do email any other time.

Now what about batching your voicemail? Rather than interrupting yourself and listening to every voicemail that comes in as soon as you see the message light flashing on your telephone, wait until you have a five- or ten-minute break in your schedule and listen to several voicemails at once. If you get a lot of voicemails, you may prefer to schedule a couple of half-hour periods during the day to deal with them. You can have a procedure for emergencies. For example, your receptionist or secretary can interrupt you about a message, or you can tell callers on your business phone to call your cell phone if they have something urgent for you.

Phone calls are another item to batch. When you do so, you can have your secretary or assistant ask the caller "Would you prefer that Mr. _____

call you back between 11:30 and 12 or between 4:30 and 5 today?" If you are calling someone and are put into their voicemail, you can include in your message the times that they can expect a return call (or the best times to reach you if they call you back).

Snail mail is another item to batch. Rather than jumping up to run out and get your mail when you hear the postman coming through the door—or, even worse, keep running out to your mailbox to see if it has arrived!--decide on a good time in the day to *schedule* the time to sort and respond to your mail. You probably have a pretty good idea of the time of day that your mail is delivered, so use that information sensibly and plan for the typical amount of time you need not only to read your mail, but to process it.

That means first trashing the junk mail and then opening the rest and dealing with it. Is it something that someone else needs to see? Route it to them. Is it something you can't make a decision about right away (an upcoming seminar that will be held at a time when you're considering going on vacation, but you want to participate if you're in town and your vacation dates aren't firmly set)? Place that seminar notice it in a tickler file so you can make the decision at a future date that still meets the enrollment deadline.

Is a piece of mail something you can answer by writing your response on the bottom of it? Go ahead and write your message and then put the letter in your outbox to be mailed. There usually is no need to compose another letter with your response. Is it something you'd like to read but don't have time for at the moment? Put it into a "to read" folder that you can keep handy for a time when you are in the mood to read.

The point is, you'll save time by batching those routine tasks rather than allowing them to interrupt you continually throughout the day. Result? You'll be able to concentrate when you're working and your productivity will soar.

GETTING CONTROL OF YOUR EMAIL

We know that email is supposed to help us save time and be more efficient. Problem is, email can turn into a monster that makes us feel frustrated and overwhelmed.

Take the following common scenario: You open your email program and see an assortment of message subject lines. You look at one and think, "I know what that's about but I can't reply now" and you move on to look at the next one. Maybe it's obvious spam, so you delete it. The next is from your mother, so you think, "It can wait—I'll read it later". You continue, maybe actually reading one or two, maybe answering one that is a "quickie"—but when you click out of your email, you've left quite a few messages in your inbox.

With this approach, your email inbox builds during the day. And every single time you go back to it, you've got to re-read (at least partially) each entry and re-decide whether to respond or to save it. With this strategy, you easily can end up with an inbox with over 100 messages (or two-or-three-hundred!). Sound familiar?

To resolve this struggle, decide that you're only going to read each entry in your inbox *once*. To do this, you have to think of your email as a virtual filing cabinet, creating a group of files that you can easily send messages to if you can't deal with them the first time they appear.

For example, you might have a file for each of your direct reports, employees or clients. You can create files for meetings or organizations you typically attend, such as "Staff Meetings", "Budget Meetings", "Human Resource Meetings" or "Rotary Club". You might have a "Continuing Education" file or a "Reference" file that contains a list of restaurants and their phone numbers to order food for meetings, a list of your coworkers/employees addresses and phone numbers, perhaps a list of vendors. And don't forget to create non-business files, perhaps your favorite sports team's schedule, family birthdays, even a "Joke" file.

A couple of files that are real time-savers are a "To Read" file and a "Wait For" file. Any articles you receive—or anything else you want to read when you have the time—send them to the "To Read" file. Then the next time you're going on an airplane, going for a doctor's visit where you know you'll have to wait, or maybe just planning an evening of reading—print out some items from your "To Read" file and have them handy in your briefcase to access when you want them.

The "Wait For" file is a wonderful way to keep from letting things "fall between the cracks" as well as giving you the satisfaction of feeling on top of things when you leave your office every day. Here's how you do it: Whenever you make a request of someone else, you blind carbon copy yourself. When the email comes back to you, you simply send it to your "Wait For" file. Then, before you leave your office for the day, you pull up that file. As you quickly review the contents, you'll see an overview of all those things you're waiting for. One or two may jump out at you because you realize that you need the information soon, signaling you either to re-email or phone the person. And, of course, you can quickly delete any item that you've already received, keeping your file current. You'll have that terrific feeling of completion knowing that you're not forgetting something important.

The basic idea behind controlling your email is that when you look at your inbox, you either respond or delete it right away—or you send it to one of your files so that it can be more easily managed when you choose to deal with it later. With this process, you're no longer spending wasted time re-reading your inbox and you've created a beautifully organized system where you can find what you want when you need it.

Now here are a few other tips for improving email management:

Turn off any sound or flashing signal that "you've got mail" on your computer. These only interrupt as you can't help but sneak a peek to see who's sending it.

Remember not to clutter other people's inboxes by hitting "reply all"; use that feature only when absolutely necessary. And create a "NTN" policy (No Thanks Needed) for internal email. When you send something to someone in your own place of employment, add "NTN" (or have it understood as a

policy that there is no need to say "Thanks, I got it" —
or send a smiley face--when someone replies to you).
All those "thank yous" can add up to lots of wasted
time for the person who has to delete them.

Finally, don't send an email when you are
upset or irritated. You may end up saying things that
you'll regret after you've had time to calm down and
think things through. Besides, if there's some type of
conflict or misunderstanding involved, it's far better
to address those issues in person rather than send a
more impersonal—and more easily misunderstood—
email.

HANDLING INTERRUPTONS

Finding yourself staying late at the office or taking work home with you? Noticing that if you get to work before anyone else arrives, you get so much more done?

That culprit sabotaging your time management could be the way you handle—or don't handle—those pesky interruptions!

As a business owner, you probably place value on being "available" to your employees. You want them to feel that they can come to you with problems, that you're not going to shut them out.

You espouse the "open door" policy. And that attitude is admirable. But you can remain "available" and still have some time to think, doing activities that require concentration. And that means closing your door.

No, you won't stay barricaded behind a closed door all—or even most—of the day. But you'll need to let your employees know that there are times when the door will be closed because you need to work with full concentration.

The next step is to tell your employees what to do when your door is closed. Do you have an assistant with whom they can leave a message? Is there a place to leave a written note? If not, you can get one of those plastic holders doctors use outside their examining rooms for patient files and attach it to (or next to) your door. Leave a small notepad inside and attach a pen that can't be removed.

Problem is, if people are used to interrupting you, they are likely to continue even when your door is closed. So you'll have to educate them. "Nancy, I'm trying something new to better manage my workload. I'll be closing my door for brief periods when I'm needing to concentrate on something, so when that happens I'm asking you to please leave me a message (specify where and how) and I'll get back to you as quickly as possible. Will you be willing to support me on this?"

Why ask for her support? Because you want her verbal agreement. People are more likely to follow through on an action if they've made a verbal commitment to do so. Also, Nancy is human. She's likely to forget a couple of times and knock on or open your door without remembering. When that happens, all you need to do is give a quick reminder ("Sorry, remember our agreement?) and she'll make a hasty exit.

What if your office doesn't have a door? If you work in an open area, place your desk so you will face a wall when you are working rather than looking at the open space. People are much more likely to begin a conversation with you (and you with them) if you are seated where there is opportunity for eye contact.

What about energy vampires—those people who always have to talk to you at length in the halls, at the water cooler, in the restroom? The ones who drop by your office too frequently and stay too long. The folks who take up your time out of neediness, insecurity or just because they love to socialize.

It helps to put a time limit on your interaction with such a person. "Tom, I have five minutes; how can I help?" But that's only half the strategy—the other half is to follow through with what you've stated. This may mean setting an appointment to talk further. Or if the person is in your office, standing up after the time you've said you could allot, saying "Sorry, I really need to stop now."

By the way, you don't have to give the other person a *reason* you need to stop. If they ask for a reason, you can say something like "I've got to make a phone call," "I've got some things it's urgent that I finish," or "I have to get ready for an appointment." While you might think it's fine to end a conversation if you have a legitimate commitment, know that it is just as okay (and necessary) to stop a conversation because you want to control your time.

People, of course, are not the only source of interruptions. What about that phone?

While there are a few businesses in which it is absolutely essential that people answer their own phones at all times, often such a policy is unnecessary. If you have an assistant, teach her to screen your calls and let her know when to interrupt you. If not, let your calls go to voice mail. You can check your messages after you've finished an activity to see if it is necessary to return the call immediately.

Otherwise, batch your return calls to a convenient time.

The point is, making yourself as interruption-free as possible sets a boundary that protects you from being continually at *someone else's* beck and call. The benefit: Control over your time—not to mention your sanity!

JOB DESCRIPTIONS

Many business owners skip a basic and very important step as they add employees to their businesses: They don't develop a job description for everyone in their organization. Or, even if they do, the employees' duties are not updated periodically. Worse yet, some employees will say "It doesn't really matter about my job description — it doesn't say anything about what I *really* do!"

The fact is, a job description *that really matches the job* is a most helpful tool for the following reasons:

It Expedites Hiring

When you're considering hiring someone for a newly-created position, formulating an accurate job description is necessary to determine the criteria you'll use for selection. Until you know specifically what the new job entails, how can you know what skills, educational requirements and job experiences to look for in a candidate? Just as important, what kinds of strengths do you want the person to have? What kind of personality will be a best fit? These are questions you can't answer until you know what the job entails.

If you're hiring someone for an existing position, it's a great time to revisit and update the job description that's already in place. Getting input from a person who currently holds that position, when appropriate, can be most helpful.

It Clarifies Expectations

Employees often complain that they just aren't told what, exactly, is expected of them on the job. Having a good job description is the first step in clarifying their roles and responsibilities.

Clear, specific language is a must. "Necessary administrative responsibilities" leaves a lot of room for interpretation.

Employees who don't have clear job descriptions can find themselves exerting lots of effort on the wrong priorities. What they think is important may not be what the boss thinks is important.

It Eliminates Conflict

A real "no-no" in the workplace is confusion about *who* is supposed to be doing *what*. Not only does this produce inefficiency due to duplication, but it is often the source of arguments or hard feelings between employees. How frustrating to work on a task or project only to find out that someone else was told to do the same thing.

Job descriptions that clearly outline the duties for each position allow a department manager and those who report to her to determine if there is confusion or overlap on specific tasks or projects. In addition to clarifying an employee's responsibilities, the manager also needs to spell out the decisions the employee is empowered to make on his own.

It Helps Determine Salary

Once you have a clear job description, it is much easier to establish salary ranges for that position. Both the responsibilities and the levels of authority are spelled out. In many instances, a job evolves and the old pay scale becomes outdated. Revising both the job description and the pay scale may prevent a valuable worker from turning in his resignation.

Let's say you are a manager who is convinced that you need either to create job descriptions for those who work for you or to update the ones that already exist. You may be thinking "Well this sounds like a lot of work; how will I ever find the time to do it?"

For a position already in existence, involve the employee who currently holds that job. Ask *him* to create or revise his job description and present it to you for further tweaking. After all, who is more likely to give you good feedback and insight about the job than the person who has been doing it? This strategy means that you're not reinventing the wheel and saves a tremendous amount of time.

If you need to create a new position, why not include others in the process? Assemble the people who will work with the new person—as well as any stakeholders—and allow them to brainstorm ideas for the job description. Not only can it make your job easier and less time-consuming, but it lets people in your organization know that you value their input.

HIRING SMART

Many small businesses do "threshold hiring": A position becomes open and due to time pressures — and perhaps uneasiness about the whole hiring process--the first seemingly eligible person who walks across the threshold is hired!

Larger companies, of course, have the luxury of having a Human Resources department with a set of procedures for hiring. But professionals and small companies usually have to wing it.

There are many personnel employment agencies and "head hunters" who can be hired to help with employee selection. This route saves a great deal of time because these agencies do the initial assessment and interviewing and present the business owner with several appropriate candidates. Yet many small companies don't want to spend the funds for these services and/or they simply prefer to do their own hiring.

So if you are a business owner who is going to do your own hiring, what can you do to make the process efficient and yet improve your odds of getting the right person?

A first critical but often overlooked step is to look closely at the responsibilities and duties of those who are already on your work team. List all the work activities appropriate to the team and ask each person to list the percentage of time he spends on each task (the total must equal 100 percent). This process helps determine what level of person to hire—or what tasks need to be reassigned internally. It also clarifies the job description for the new hire.

For example, a law firm may think it needs to hire another paralegal but discovers that the paralegal it already has is spending time opening mail, running copies, doing word processing and answering the phone rather than doing productive, billable work. It may be more appropriate for the firm to hire a secretary to do these tasks and free the paralegal to use her talents working on documents, acquiring records, and performing other tasks for which she is trained.

The next step is to perform a "labor needs" assessment. This involves listing the different tasks the new hire will be expected to perform and then deciding which personality characteristics the position requires. For instance, will the new person be working with clients? If so, he will need to have good people skills. For someone who will be doing research or filing with little or no client contact, a person who is detail-oriented will be best suited for the position.

After determining the kind of work to be done and the personality characteristics for an ideal match, consider the minimum level of experience you want the new hire to have. What kind of work might the person have done before that would make her an instant asset and require minimal training? It may be worth it in the long run to hire a more experienced person at a higher salary who can "hit the ground running" rather than to get an inexperienced person who will require extensive training.

Next, consider the skills you want the new hire to have. For support positions, knowledge about specific types of software and office equipment might be important. Skill assessment of typing, grammar, filing, attention to detail and proofreading are also necessary. For higher level positions, consider requesting a work sample prior to making a final hiring decision. A personality assessment may also be helpful. When it is clear which kinds of assessments are appropriate, decide which ones, if any, will be done for screening purposes and which ones will be saved for final candidates after interviews.

Prior to interviewing it is most helpful to prepare an interview evaluation form that allows the hiring person(s) to compare candidates on key criteria. Categories may include education, experience, practical knowledge, communication skills, composure/overall impression, motivation, appearance, etc. Each interviewee can be rated by the interviewer as "outstanding", "above average", "average" and "below average" on each criterion, making it much simpler to make a final selection among candidates.

If others in the company are going to be working closely with the new hire, allow them an opportunity to meet, conduct their own informal interviews and have input into the process. This not only makes current employees feel valued but also ensures that they will be supportive of the new hire (since they had a say in the selection and would not want to be wrong).

No matter how pleased you are with a candidate, reference checks are still a must. Better to spend the extra time being safe rather than sorry.

Finally, consider sending a "thank you" note to every applicant. While it is common these days for this courtesy to be omitted, think of the reputation your business creates when it cares enough to take this extra step.

WELCOMING YOUR NEW EMPLOYEE

Do you remember how it felt to start a new job? Did you find your "first day" interesting and exciting? Did your boss and your peers try to make you feel comfortable and glad to be there? Or did you experience a "first day" that made you wonder if you'd made a huge mistake accepting the job?

It's a no-brainer that, as a business owner, you want any new employee to feel welcome when she begins working for you—no matter how big or how small your business. But does your behavior match your good intentions? Do you have an orientation process that is well-planned and effective?

A successful orientation should not only ensure that new people feel welcome, but also makes sure that they have the tools and equipment they need to do their jobs as well as information about company culture and policies. So let's look at some tips for creating a "first day on the job" (and the 90 days to follow) that your new person will remember with positive feelings.

Before the new person arrives, it is a good idea to let the other people in your company know he is coming and the job he will be doing. An email telling something about the person—especially to team members that will interact with her—is helpful in alerting people to expect a new face.

Obviously, you'll want a newcomer to have a comfortable and efficient work station or office. This would include a telephone (and a list of extensions), an up-and-running computer fully loaded with applicable software (and passwords), and a variety of office supplies (paper, envelopes, pens/pencils, scissors, scotch tape, highlighters, paper clips, white out, sticky pads, ruler, stapler and staple remover, a hole punch, in-basket, file folder rack, folders, etc.). Make sure the desk chair offers good back support and has a plastic mat under it if needed.

Prepare a New Employee Packet that includes a company Policies and Procedures Manual, information on health insurance and other benefits and financial forms (for withholding, 401-K, etc.). Create a personal profile form (all contact information for the new employee, birthday, etc.) for the new person to complete.

Be sure to assign the newcomer a "Buddy" for the first day whose goal is to create a sense of belonging for the new hire and to be the point person for any questions. The "Buddy" will introduce the new person to other employees, talk about the company history and culture, and discuss the importance of the new person's job to the company, team and customers. This is also a good time to familiarize her with the policy for reporting absences and late arrivals.

The "Buddy" also would provide a tour of the facilities, including a general overview and location of restrooms and office supplies. Touring the break room or kitchen also provides a good opportunity to inform the person about policies for storing food in the refrigerator, dishwashing, making coffee, etc. Most important, the "Buddy" will go to lunch with the newcomer so he does not have to eat alone the first day.

If possible, set up a lunch with team members sometime within the new arrival's first week. At the

"Welcome Lunch", she can be asked to share a bit about her life—as can other team members.

The supervisor or manager of a new hire needs to make sure that expectations for "doing a good job" are very clear and that the person is set up for a "win" by being given work that he already is comfortable with and can execute well. As the person is ready, more challenging work can be added.

Setting specific goals for the new person to accomplish every 30 days gives structure and allows both the manager and the new hire to get feedback about whether the new person is meeting or exceeding job expectations. People like to know where they stand, especially in a new situation, so a formal evaluation process during the usual 90-day probation period is a good idea.

The first 90 days on the job also provides a good opportunity to benchmark the new person's skills and determine a training track that will meet her needs. Training can be provided via job "shadowing" (the person observes someone else doing a designated task), company classes, independent seminars, programs at conferences, mentoring, etc.

Planning ahead for the arrival of a new employee by having a clear "welcoming" and orientation process reveals a business whose owner and managers are both thoughtful as well as efficient.

CONSIDER THE GENERATION GAPS

Just about any business you're in, you'll find a common challenge: Conflict between the "older" versus the "younger" employees. But the problem isn't really that simple. Actually, there currently are five generations in the workplace—each with its own background, values, beliefs and characteristics.

The Silent Generation (Radio Babies)

Born between 1930 and 1945, this generation gets its name from the fact that they grew up with the radio as the most common form of home entertainment. They mowed the lawn with a push mower, listened to Ricky Nelson on the radio, knew how to entertain themselves without a television and remember the first TVs as being black and white.

They had heroes to admire; many fought in World War II. Communism was the enemy. They tend to be fiscally prudent, conservative, and very loyal to their employers and employees. They survived the Great Depression of the early1930s, making it easy to understand their emphasis on job security as well as the fact that job-hopping is not a concept they embrace. If they use a computer, their biggest fear is that they'll break it.

The Baby Boomers

This generation was born between 1946 and 1964. They knew Elvis before he wore sequins, used a typewriter to write their term papers, watched *Leave It To Beaver* on television, remember Woodstock, listened to the Beatles, and watched man's first trip to the moon.

Boomers have witnessed several revolutions in America—from the advent of the sexual revolution with women gaining access to "the pill" to the blossoming of the civil rights movement. Many fought in (or protested) the Vietnam War. They were told by their parents that they could have anything they dreamed of and that getting a college education was the vehicle to a better lifestyle. They are often stereotyped as aging flower children from the Sixties who sold out to become the "suits" of the Eighties, becoming ambitious and materialistic. They believe heartily in The American Dream and maintain (at least some of the time) that they can "have it all."

Generation X (Gen X)

Born between 1965 and 1976, this generation rode backwards in a station wagon on family trips, know who shot J.R. on television, used a rotary phone, actually played records, and recall the advent of Atari, *ET* and the first *Star Wars* movie. They've seen technology emerge and grow from records to eight-track tapes, cassettes, CDs, DVDs, MP3s and, of course, computers.

They've watched the Internet take off as well as the dawn of voice mail, walkmans, beepers, cell phones, PDAs, laptops, GPSs and ipads. Most own one computer, some two or three. They were the original "latch key" kids and watched their parents get "let go" from the corporations to which they had been so loyal. They learned that politics never solved anything (and often made things worse), and grew up scared due to the threat of nuclear war, terrorist attacks, AIDS and Watergate. They see no point in "paying dues" to get ahead and reject the notion that people should sacrifice their lives to their work.

Millennials (Generation Y)

People born between 1977 and 1991, Generation Y, is often referred to as "Generation X on steroids!" Three times the size of the Gen Xers, they grew up with similar circumstances to Generation X (dual-income parents, daycare, divorce) but were subjected to different parenting styles. For discipline, spankings were viewed as child abuse and time outs were in. Parents sought to protect their children from the world's pitfalls.

This generation has at least thought about piercing something besides their ears, has always known about Cable TV and remote controls, used a computer about the time they learned to read, grew up on video games and has always made popcorn in a microwave. They are very conscious of preserving our environment, are committed to social causes, are very accepting of every form of diversity (racial, ethnic, sexual orientation, gender, etc.) and express themselves creatively in their appearance (body jewelry, brightly colored hair, etc.). They tend to be much more against alcohol, drugs and premarital sex than either Boomers or Gen Xers. Their number one concern is personal safety (think school shootings and terrorism).

Network Generation (Generation Z)

This is the generation that is just starting to enter the workforce. Born in the early 90s, they've grown up with the influence of the World Wide Web. They are post-Cold War and the fall of the Soviet Union, but experienced 9/11. They grew up as masters of technology; they've grown up texting, instant messaging, using smart phones, ipads and GPSs and watching U Tube. A favorite form of communication is social networking, and they share their views and ideas on a variety of media.

This generation has grown up quickly, yet been somewhat overprotected by being chauffeured to their activities. They are great multi-taskers, want to "connect" with others, and are very accepting of globalization and all types of diversity. Given their current reality as they worry about money for college and/or getting a job, they are thought to be fragile and somewhat needy.

Generation Z has had to deal with a decade of war and economic uncertainty. Dubious about their futures, they've entered the workplace in a recession. Their mainly Millennial parents grew up in good economic times and thought the world was their oyster. They looked to their own individual needs and wants at work and, if they disliked the policies of their employers, they'd simply quit and find another job more to their liking. But their children, Generation Zers, have such concerns about being employed that they are much more likely to accept unpleasant policies from their managers. Because they've spent so much of their lives in front of a screen, it is believed that they will have more difficulty with face-to-face people interaction. Rather than telling their boss they disagree, they'll put their opinion on Facebook.

With such variety of life-experiences, is it any wonder that the generations have difficulty understanding one another—at work or anywhere else?

There are books written about what each generation needs to understand about the others, but the starting place for resolving generation-inspired conflict is to understand that each one of us is a product to some extent of how we were parented and, even more importantly, what was going on in the world while we were growing up. Considering these factors can give the business owner a starting place for understanding the values and viewpoints of each generation without making anyone "wrong".

Sometimes, just having a presentation about generational differences in the workplace helps all employees better understand one another's behavior and attitudes, increasing their understanding and tolerance for differing points of view

PERFORMANCE APPRAISALS: THE COMMON MISTAKES!

A performance appraisal is a tool to give employees formal feedback about their job performance. Whether you've been on the "giving" or the "receiving" end, you've probably had your share of frustration with the entire experience.

Let's take a look at the common mistakes that can turn the appraisal process into a management nightmare:

Don't Give One!

People need and deserve to get feedback about how they are perceived by their bosses. But without a performance appraisal system in place, managers tend to put off this important task for several reasons. Other job demands may seem to be a higher priority—there doesn't seem to be time available in an already time-stressed work environment. Or the manager may see the employee as doing a great job and assumes that he already knows it and doesn't need any confirmation. Conversely, the manager may know the employee is not doing so well, but doesn't want to confront the unpleasant reality.

When employees don't get formal evaluations at least on a yearly basis, whatever assumptions they might be making about how they and their work are perceived can be off the mark. Whether they're correct or not, they need to know the truth.

Don't Have The Business Owner's Support For The Process.

A business owner needs to believe in the value of the appraisal process and commit to making it happen. And that means making managers or supervisors accountable for formal evaluations of their employees.

So why might the managers and supervisors resist this process? Perhaps they fear that the business owner is intolerant of mistakes; they don't want to "look bad" themselves and so they are motivated to hide employee problems. They may dislike the confrontation that comes with having to give an employee negative feedback. They may fear that they can't back up their perceptions because they've failed to do the necessary documentation. They may have neglected to be straight with their employees and now dread the backlash that can come with the employee's saying "Well, why didn't you tell me this before now?"

It is the business owner who needs to model the process, evaluating her own direct reports. This makes it clear that everyone in the company gets an evaluation, not just the employees at the bottom of the employee ladder.

Don't Prepare--Wing It!

A good performance evaluation requires some planning. The person giving it must be able to back up his statements by citing instances of observed behavior, not just subjective impressions. Even when the message is "You're doing an outstanding job!", some specifics need to be cited so the employee is clear on why she is getting an outstanding evaluation.

Don't Get The Employee's Feedback Prior To The Evaluation.

Employees feel valued when they are asked to fill out their own performance evaluations prior to their managers or business owner's doing so—even if they complain about having to do it! This gives them the opportunity to mention accomplishments throughout the year—some of which their boss(es) may not have known or may have forgotten, and allows the person doing the evaluation to see how employees perceive their own performances. The bigger the discrepancy in perceptions, the more time will be needed for the actual evaluation meeting. If there is good agreement, the evaluator's job will be much easier and not require as much time.

Don't Tell The Truth.

Many business owners and managers dread giving employees negative feedback. They want to be kind and not be labeled as "bad guys." However, not being straight with an employee really does her a disservice as it denies her the opportunity to correct behaviors/perceptions of which she may be totally unaware and which may cause career derailment in the future.

Don't Create A Clear Action Plan.

An important part of any performance evaluation is to set some clear goals for the future. This is particularly important if an employee has some weak areas to correct. Goals must be specific and measurable. For example, rather than the vague "You need to improve your attitude", say something like "You need to eliminate sarcasm about company policies" or "You need to address your complaint directly to the person with whom you have a problem rather than talking to others about that person's behavior."

Make Judgmental Remarks.

When giving someone negative feedback, stick to behaviors rather than making judgments. "You're having difficulty getting to work on time" is matter-of-fact but delivers the message; "You're irresponsible" is a judgment. Likewise, "Your production is not meeting the assigned goal" is much better than "You're getting lazy."

Make The Evaluation A Dead End.

Some people heave a sigh of relief when a performance appraisal is over and think "Thank goodness this is over for another year!" But the appraisal is part of a *process*, not an end it itself. Although formal appraisals may be given only once a year, there should be no surprises to the employees when they are given their evaluations. This means that throughout the year, they need to be given informal feedback on how they are doing, especially if their behavior or skills need improvement.

By avoiding these common mistakes, both the "evaluators" and the "evaluatees" can look forward to the performance appraisal process. Employees almost always want to do well, and they respect the business owner, manager, or supervisor who acknowledges them for their strengths and are clear with them about what can be improved.

RESOLVING THOSE WORKPLACE CONFLICTS!

It happens in every workplace setting where there are two or more people. Somehow there's a misperception, a tension, or an outright disagreement. It can be between any two people—boss and employee, peers, team members, staff—or it can escalate to involve entire departments or teams. Sometimes it's labeled a "communication problem" and sometimes it's called an out-and-out conflict.

So how do you resolve these difficulties that can eat up so much time in productivity and/or cause emotional discomfort (if not grief) to those involved?

There are two common mistakes that are often made in these situations. First, people simply don't acknowledge that anything is wrong. Not wanting "confrontation," they ignore the difficulty and hope it resolves itself. Their motto is "Just give it time and it will take care of itself" or "Let's wait and see—these things have a way of working themselves out." What happens realistically is that the conflict often festers and goes underground only to raise its head later and with more force.

The second mistake is to tackle the situation by pointing fingers and/or by trying to enlist others in a blaming game. The aim is to make somebody "wrong," thus making someone else "right." Instead of going to the person with whom they have a problem, they go to others to rally their causes.

A more helpful approach is to confront the other person directly—but in a non-confrontational way—using the following five-step approach:

First, begin the conversation with *"In the situation when....."* For example, imagine that someone criticized you when others could hear what was said. Rather than going to that person and saying "Yesterday when you criticized me in the hallway..." you say *"In the situation* yesterday when we were in the hallway and you were talking to me about the X project...." This is a less blaming approach because you're talking about a *situation* rather than making a personal attack.

Second, after stating the situation, you add *"I felt...."* In our example, you might continue with *"I felt* embarrassed."* Just make a simple statement about your feelings.

Third, explain *why* you felt the way you felt by continuing with *"because...."* "In the situation yesterday when we were in the hallway and you were talking to me about the X project, I felt embarrassed *because* other people overheard your comments."

Fourth, *be silent.* Don't say anything. This is the other person's opportunity to explain himself. Very often, he will apologize for his actions in some way. He might say "You know, I realized after I made those comments that other people could hear me. I'm so sorry; I didn't intend for that to happen." In this case, you understand one another and the problem, hopefully, is solved.

If the other person justifies his behavior or his comments don't lead to a discussion that resolves the problem, you're left with Step 5: *Negotiate a solution or make a request.* "I understand that you weren't trying to embarrass me, but I request that in the future when you are critiquing me, you invite me to your office or some other place where we can have a private conversation."

Most of the time this five-step process works well. But what if the other person refuses your request? Hopefully, you can simply agree to disagree and to move on, aware of one another's feelings on the matter.

And what if you are the one being confronted? An employee comes to you with a complaint about something you did or said. The worst mistake is to become angry or defensive in your attempt to justify what you did or didn't do. If there is an explanation, give it—but you can still apologize for the other person's feeling upset even if you believe your behavior was appropriate. "How would you prefer I handle something like this?" or "What could we do differently so we can have a more positive result?" are helpful questions to create a dialogue rather than an argument.

If you are at fault or agree with the other person that you could have handled the situation in a different way, then admit it. Let's face it—we all have bad days, make mistakes and behave in ways we wish we hadn't. Not to mention that there will always be differing points of view about an issue.

It's not the conflict that is the problem—it's the way you handle it that matters.

REWARDING YOUR EMPLOYEES

Business owners know the value of providing incentives and perks for their employees, but too often, they think only in terms of money. Not that their employees don't like money (it's probably their first choice), but monetary gifts can be expensive, especially during a struggling economy. Even if a business is able to offer money as a bonus some of the time, there are numerous other types of prizes that allow employees to be rewarded more frequently.

The problem is that other types of incentives often miss the mark in terms of employee satisfaction. Someone decides "Wouldn't it be nice to reward our best employees with a gift certificate for a massage? Or a bottle of good wine? Or an appointment to have a car detailed?"

But not everyone likes massages. For example, people may be self-conscious about their bodies or may not like being touched because they were sexually abused in the past. The person receiving a gift of wine may be a recovering alcoholic, or may be a Scotch drinker. And some people don't find having their car detailed to be a big motivator. The point is, why not *ask* employees how they would like to be rewarded from a series of choices?

Employees can be given a simple form with categories, such as: spa services, restaurant coupons, tickets to movies or sporting events, department store credits, flowers, food items, electronics, etc. Each category can have several offerings. For example, spa services might have mani/pedis, facials and massage. Sport events might include choices of tickets for various home teams in your city: basketball, football, soccer, hockey, baseball, etc. If the employee picks "restaurant coupons", she might be asked to list her three favorite restaurants. Food items might include chocolates, deli items, pies or cakes, specialty meats, etc. Employees also can be given a catalogue and a gift certificate, allowing them to pick the item of their choice.

An often overlooked--but very popular reward—is time off. The ability to leave work at noon on a Friday or to take a paid day off is a favorite of many employees. And, of course, there's the ever-popular ability to park in a highly desired spot!

The point is that employees really appreciate the business owner who customizes rewards to their preferences.

THE COMPANY RETREAT

Ever noticed the number of eye rolls when an employer announces it is time for another company retreat? People are thinking "Well, there goes another day shot when I have work I need to be doing!" or "Not again! I don't need another day being bored!"

Of course, that's not exactly the response you want as a business owner. You see the retreat as an opportunity to get away from business-as-usual, to build esprit-de-corps, to work on goals for the following year, to solve some problems and/or to update people on critical issues. And maybe even to have some fun in the process.

Problem is, even with the best of intentions, many company retreats turn out to be big disappointments for everyone. Not to mention being a large, non-productive expense.

To have a dynamic retreat—the kind people will leave saying "Wow! This was great!"—the critical key is *planning*. So often a retreat is thrown together at the last minute, perhaps with the hiring of a speaker on a topic the retreat planner thinks will be interesting. An agenda is put together, but with little pre-work or genuine preparation.

Where will the retreat be held? The worst place is in the conference room—or anywhere in the building in which the business is located. There is simply too much temptation for the attendees to dash out to make a phone call, check their voicemails and emails, or do some office work. A hotel meeting room or other conference facility off premises is better. Best is a relaxing location out of town, especially if the retreat is to last more than a day; then there's a true feeling of getting-away-from-it-all which encourages a focus on the retreat agenda, creative thinking and camaraderie.

Careful attention needs to be given to the purpose of the retreat—what are the attendees supposed to come away with? Answering this critical question is necessary in order to know what pre-work needs to be done. For example, let's say staff morale seems to be a problem. Typically, this topic could become an agenda item for the retreat. But how much more effective it would be to have the staff fill out a survey in advance. Then when the topic of morale is discussed at the retreat, the data can be given out and discussion can focus on facts rather than conjecture.

Perhaps cash flow is an issue. Having a printout of accounts receivables for the past year to give out to attendees can allow a more targeted discussion of possible remedies.

Determining the retreat objectives also will dictate who should attend the retreat. Should it be the owner and managers? Just a particular department? Just the staff? Is it more appropriate to have everyone?

Perhaps a half day can be used for one group and the other half for another. Or maybe the management team spends the first part of the day together and then is joined by staff later in the day. Should spouses be invited and have separate activities while the attendees are meeting?

If teambuilding and renewal are desired, plan some downtime with recreational options. Many retreat facilities offer golf, horseback riding, hiking, tubing or spa services. If you're spending the night, would people like to bring board games or CDs for informal evening activities. What about a talent show? Or an award ceremony (humorous or serious)?

Of course, you can have a retreat with excellent content, creative ideas, good problem solving and even some fun and still have participants leave feeling that nothing substantive was accomplished. For this not to occur, it is critical to have action items—and a method of accountability—to implement when everyone gets back to the office.

To be effective, the action items need to specify *who* will do *what* by *when*. For example, rather than concluding "We will start working on establishing a mentoring program", the action items might be as follows:

- Mark, Juan, Lily and Sandra will form a Mentoring Committee to begin meeting bi-weekly starting next month;
- Andrew and Sue will research current information on mentoring programs during the next 30 days and present their findings to the Mentoring Committee at the committee's second meeting.
- The Mentoring Committee will present their proposal for a company Mentoring Program to the Executive Committee at the Fall Quarterly meeting.

Finally, how will accountability be created? Will it be a task designated to an individual? Will there be another retreat in six months where progress will be measured?

With careful planning, your retreat can be what it was designed to be: A catalyst for a refocusing of energies, a clarification of objectives and priorities, a realignment with vision, a learning experience, an opportunity to share fun and relaxation with colleagues and *a commitment to action*. Most importantly, you and your employees will feel the retreat was time well spent

TAKING CARE OF MOI

How nice are you being to a very special person—*you*. If you're like most people, you spend a majority of your energy focusing on what needs to be done for everyone else—your significant other, your kids, your family, your friends, your business, and the various organizations you support. And what often gets left out of the mix is time to focus on yourself.

The truth is, we're all like bags of chocolate chip cookies! If your bag is full and brimming over with cookies, you've got lots to give to everyone. But if you're down to just a few lousy crumbs in the bottom of your bag, you're stressed out, cranky and more likely to succumb to stress-related illnesses.

So the trick is to keep your bag full. But how?

Set Boundaries

You can't be everything to everyone. And you can't be available all the time. Set up some simple ground rules that will keep you sane. For example, no phone calls during dinner. And no calls after a certain time at night (let the answering machine do the work for you and refuse to call back unless it is a true emergency).

Perhaps you set aside 30 minutes to an hour every evening just to connect with your spouse or significant other. If you have young children, this time would be after their bedtime; with older youngsters, they can learn that this is "grown-up time" and entertain themselves or do homework. Maybe you set aside 30 minutes just for yourself, retreating to your bedroom or a favorite spot to read, watch the television, phone a friend, or take a nap, letting the other adult in the house deal with the kids during that time.

Get Used To Saying "No!"

Quit saying "yes" to everything you're asked to do. If you have this tendency, vow to give yourself 24 hours before committing yourself to anything. For example, "I need to sleep on that to make my decision, so I'll call you tomorrow" or "That sounds good but I need to give it some thought; I'll let you know my decision tomorrow."

Or learn a technique to say "no" by saying "yes": When someone asks you to do something, tell them "Let me tell you what I can do" — and then proceed to agree to something that is *much less* than what the person requested. For example, let's say it's seven in the evening and your child's teacher calls. She tells you that the class is having a bake sale the next day and they're short on items — and you make such wonderful Italian cream cakes. Could you just whip one up and bring it in the morning?" You respond with something like "Let me tell you what I can do. I have some frozen lemon bars in the fridge and I'd be happy to send those in the morning."

Practice declining gracefully until it feels natural and your voice sounds matter-of-fact but confident: "You know, I'd love to help you out, but I just have too much on my plate right now. I'm going to have to say 'no'." Or simply, "I'm sorry, but I'm just not able to do that." Period. You don't need to explain yourself and give reasons. If the other person

113

continues to press by asking why you can't comply, say something like, "It's just not in the cards this week!" or "I promised myself I wouldn't accept one more commitment this week/month." Then stick to your guns.

Remember, "no" is actually a complete sentence!

Trim The Extracurricular Activities

Maybe in the interest of business networking, you've joined numerous organizations that are now sapping your time and energy. If you find yourself getting ready to attend one of these meetings and thinking, "Gee, I wish I didn't have to go to this," it may be time to get out.

If an organization doesn't bring you business or touch your soul, it's time to leave. If you hold an office in such an organization, make a promise to yourself to leave after your obligation is fulfilled. Trim the dead wood and devote your energy, time, and attention to those activities that really matter to you.

Take Time For Yourself

What are the activities that you enjoy doing "just because"? It could be reading, taking a bubble bath, fiddling in your garden, working on a craft project, playing with your dog, going for a walk, sipping a glass of wine on the patio and watching the sunset, exercising, meditating—the list of possibilities is endless. Whatever it is, arrange the time to do one of them every day. Taking 10 to 30 minutes for these kinds of activities will recharge your physical and emotional batteries.

In addition to these daily "recharges", think of some rejuvenating activities that take a couple of hours and plan to do those on a weekly basis. Go to a movie, have lunch with a friend, take a class, visit a museum, get a pedicure—again, the list is endless.

And while you're at it, plan your next vacation now (if you haven't done so already). Put it on your calendar and work your schedule around it rather than waiting for "the perfect time" that always gets postponed. A sprinkling of mini-vacations also happen more often if they're scheduled in advance!

By taking care of yourself, you're going to be a better business owner, friend, spouse, parent—and human being.

ABOUT THE AUTHOR

Judi Craig, Ph.D., MCC is an Executive and Business Coach in San Antonio, TX, and President of COACH SQUARED. She holds the Master Certified Coach designation, the highest industry certification granted by the International Coach Federation. She coaches business owners, executives and managers in over 18 industries on enhancing leadership, improving "people skills", facilitating powerful communication, increasing business/sales and taking charge of their careers. She also coaches professionals on re-engineering their practices by increasing their incomes, cutting their work hours, solving their staffing headaches and taking better care of their clients. Always looking to bring proven resources to her clients, she formed COACH SQUARED ONLINE in 2012, providing an E-Learning Marketing Center that gives small business owners all the tools and resources they need to skyrocket their revenues and profits.

Dr. Craig is also a clinical psychologist who has had her own successful private clinical practice for over 30 years. A frequent guest on national radio and television, she has been interviewed on over 100 radio stations and has been a guest on Larry King

Live, The Today Show, NBC News, CBS News, Geraldo and other nationally-televised programs. As a keynote speaker, she has addressed audiences as diverse as the executives of CBS Television to the rescue and service workers of the Oklahoma City bombing and currently gives presentations and retreats on a variety of coaching-related business topics.

Dr. Craig is a former syndicated columnist, the author of five nationally published books and a Master Practitioner in Neurolinguistic Programming. She is the author of the e-book Help! I Lost My Job! (www.lost-my-job.com) and wrote the Biz Coach column in the bi-monthly SA Woman (4 years) and the Practice Boosters column in The Complete Lawyer online magazine (two years). Her latest book is Brain-Switch (2012).

Dr. Craig received her Bachelor of Arts degree from Southern Methodist University (Phi Beta Kappa) and her Master's and Doctorate Degrees from the University of Wisconsin. She is a graduate of both Coach U and Corporate Coach U, and served on the Corporate Coach U faculty for eight years.

To Contact Dr. Craig
Phone: 210-824-3391
Email: judi@coachsquared.com
For More Information
www.coachsquaredonline.com
www.coachsquared.com

www.ingramcontent.com/pod-product-compliance
Lightning Source LLC
Chambersburg PA
CBHW071214200326
41519CB00018B/5513